Mapping

Heather C. Hudak

WEIGL PUBLISHERS INC.

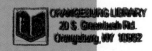

Published by Weigl Publishers Inc.
350 5th Avenue, Suite 3304, PMB 6G
New York, NY 10118-0069

Website: www.weigl.com

Library of Congress Cataloging-in-Publication Data

Hudak, Heather C., 1975-
  Mapping / Heather C. Hudak.
      p. cm. -- (Social studies essential skills)
  Includes index.
  ISBN 978-1-59036-761-2 (lib. bdg. : alk. paper) -- ISBN 978-1-59036-762-9 (soft cover : alk. paper)
 1. Cartography--Juvenile literature. 2. Maps--Juvenile literature. 3. Map reading--Juvenile literature. I. Title.
  GA105.6.H83 2008
  912--dc22
                              2007024013

Printed in the United States of America
1 2 3 4 5 6 7 8 9 0 11 10 09 08 07

Editor: Heather C. Hudak
Design: Terry Paulhus

Photo credits: Courtesy of the U.S. Geological Survey: page 7 bottom right.

Table of Contents

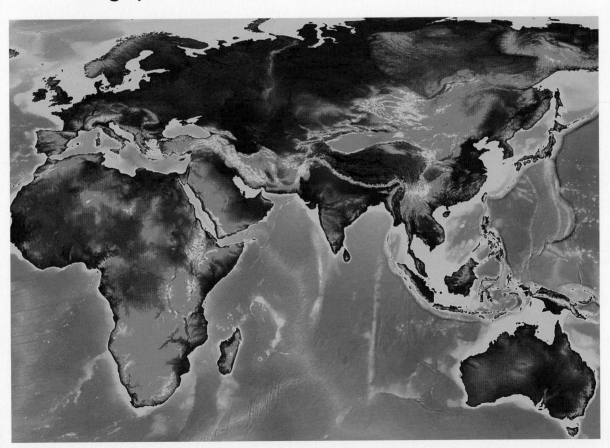

What is a Map?

When a view of Earth's surface is shown on a flat surface, the image is called a map. A map may show the entire surface of Earth, or it may show only certain parts of Earth's surface. Maps also show where places are in relation to each other in terms of distance, size, and direction.

This map shows the position of the seven **continents** and five oceans. Does it show all or part of Earth's surface?

Now, look at this map. Does it show all or part of Earth's surface? Can you name the countries found in this part of the world?

Finding Places on a Map

Using the map below, find the state where you live. Then, draw a map showing just your state.

On your map, be sure to include the name of the state. You can show that states's borders. What are the names of the bordering states?

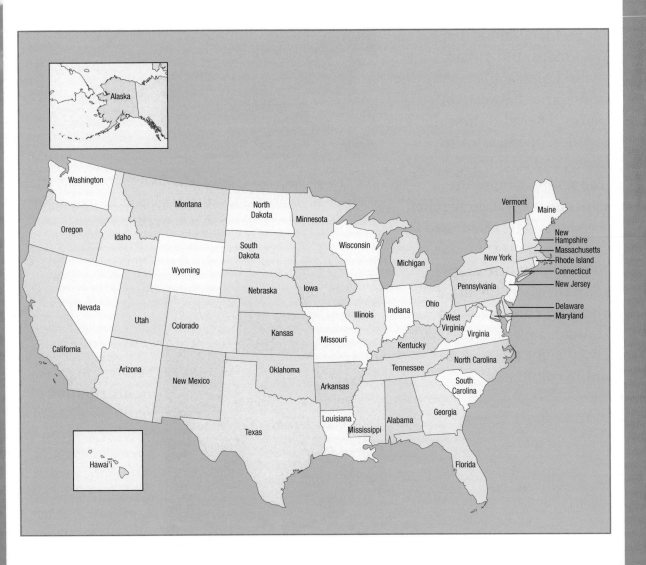

Types of Maps

There are many types of maps. Each type shows something different about Earth's surface. This is because a single map can only show a few things about an area. The same place can have many types of maps, depending on what needs to be shown. Every map has a subject. Two main types of maps are general reference maps and thematic maps.

General reference maps show where different features are located. Four types of general reference maps are political maps, topographic maps, road maps, and physical maps. Political maps show the boundaries between different places. They also show the location of cities, towns, states, and countries. Topographic maps use **contour** lines to show **relief**. Road maps are often used to find directions from one place to another. These maps indicate where the main roads and highways run through a place. They may cover a city, town, or an entire country.

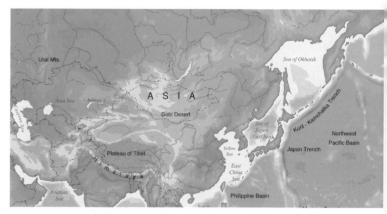

A physical map is a type of general reference map. It displays landforms, such as rivers, lakes, or mountains. Each landform is shown in a different color.

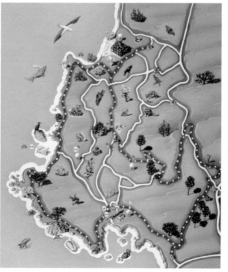

*Thematic maps show the **distribution** of something that can be found in a specific area. A resource map is a type of thematic map. It uses symbols to show where crops grow or where minerals are mined.*

Knowing the Type of Map

Look at the four maps below. Can you tell what type of map each one is?

1. Road map
2. Political map

3. Physical map
4. Topographic map

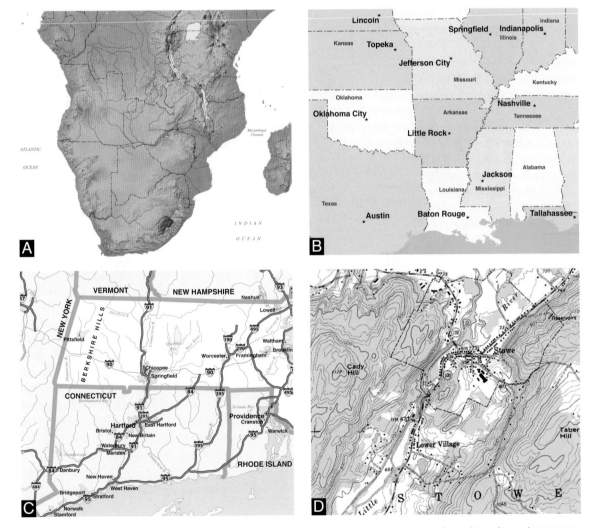

Learning to Read a Legend

Maps often use special symbols and colors to represent different items. These items are then explained in the legend, or key. The legend uses words to explain what each symbol means.

The legend provides the information that is needed to understand the map. On a political map, a star or dot may represent a city. Sometimes symbols, such as different colors or lines, are used. Blue is often used to show bodies of water, such as lakes and rivers.

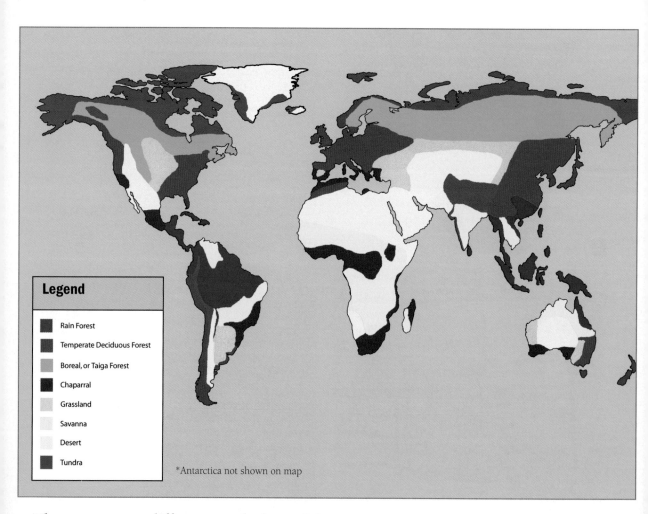

Legend

- Rain Forest
- Temperate Deciduous Forest
- Boreal, or Taiga Forest
- Chaparral
- Grassland
- Savanna
- Desert
- Tundra

*Antarctica not shown on map

There are many different symbols on this map. Look at the legend to see what each symbol represents.

Making a Legend

This is a hand-drawn map showing the village where its artist lives. Notice how the legend explains the drawing. Draw a map of your classroom. Begin by drawing the shape of the room on a piece of paper. Then, use symbols to show the location of objects in the classroom. You might use small squares to show the location of desks or triangles for the location of computers.

Once you have completed your map, make a legend. Be sure to explain what each symbol represents.

LEGEND

 Roads

 Housing

 Rivers

Learning about Landforms and Bodies of Water

Landforms are the natural features of Earth's surface. There are many types of landforms, such as mountains, canyons, valleys, plateaus, deserts, **archipelagos**, and plains. Landforms are made by erosion and **tectonic** activity. Forms of erosion, such as wind and rain, shape Earth's surface. As the elements move across an area, they remove part of the surface. The pieces settle in another place.

Bodies of water are another feature of Earth's surface. There are many types of bodies of water, including oceans, lakes, rivers, and streams.

Landforms and bodies of water can be shown on a map in many ways. They may appear as special colors or symbols. Usually, relief lines or shadings are used to show the height and depth of landforms. Relief shows the difference in height between places on a map.

To read more about different types of landforms and bodies of water, visit **www.earthkam.ucsd.edu/ public/students/activities/ landformations**.

Using relief gives the map a three-dimensional look. This makes it easier to tell what the terrain or landscape actually looks like.

Identifying Landforms

Look at the pictures of the landforms and bodies of water below. Then, try answering these questions for each of the pictures. You may need to research online or visit your library to find out more about different types of landforms.

1. How was this landform or body of water created?

2. Find out where each of these landforms or bodies of water are located. Then, use an **atlas** to find its location on a map. Look at the legend, and explain how it is represented.

Mount Everest

Grand Canyon

Nile River

Working to Scale

Earth's surface is much larger than it appears on a map. Mapmakers, or cartographers, must draw parts of Earth much smaller than they actually are. This is called working to scale.

Mapmakers include a scale on each map to show how big each feature on the map is in relation to its actual size. It also shows the relative distance between two points on Earth and the same two points on the map. All features on a map are drawn using the same scale.

There are many types of scales. Some scales use fractions or ratios to express size. These are called representative fraction scales. The ratio 1:10,000 means that one unit of measure on the map is equal to 10,000 of the same units of measure on Earth. Sometimes, scales are used to express size in terms of numbers. On a resource map, a 1:10,000 scale might mean that the symbol for one cow represents 10,000 cows. On these scales, the first number is always "1." The second number changes, depending on the map.

Other scales use a line to show distance. A 1-inch line may be equal to 1,000 miles. The map reader uses a ruler to determine the length of the line and the distance between points. This is called a graphic scale.

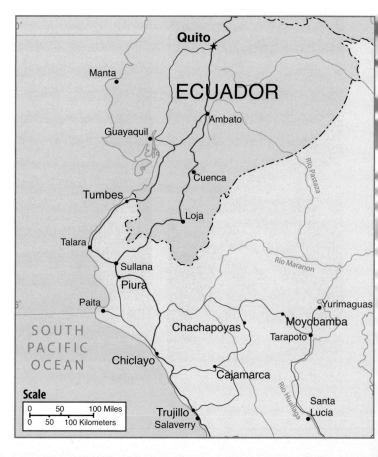

Finding the Distance

Look at the two maps printed below. Map 1 shows the entire continent of Europe. Map 2 shows only a few countries in Europe. It has more detail about each place. Use the two maps to answer the following questions.

1. On Map 1, find the location of the countries that are shown on Map 2.
2. What type of scale is used for each map?
3. Measure the distance between two points on Map 1. Then, measure the distance between the same two points on Map 2. Use the scale for each map to see if the distance is the same.

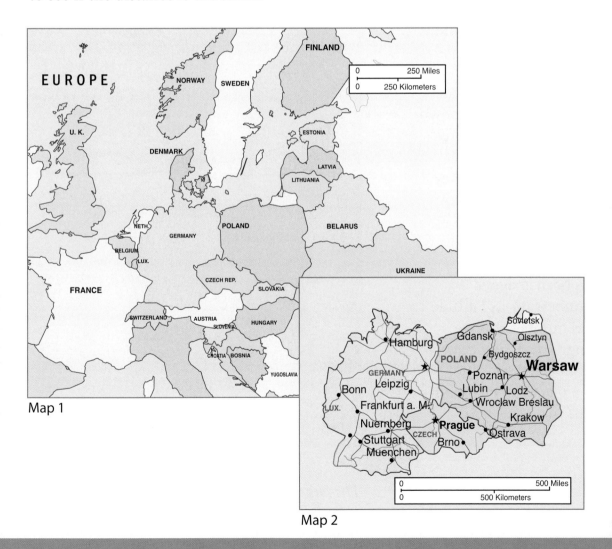

Map 1

Map 2

What is a Geographic Grid?

A geographic grid is used to locate places on a map. This type of grid is made up of **latitude** and **longitude** lines.

Latitude lines run horizontally along the map. They are **parallel** to the equator. Longitude, or meridian, lines run vertically across the map. They are **perpendicular** to the equator.

Latitude and longitude lines cross each other. A number, or coordinate, is given to the place where they cross. Latitude and longitude measurements are shown in degrees. Each degree is divided into 60 minutes (60'). Minutes are often divided into 60 seconds (60").

Each place on Earth has been assigned numbers for its latitude and numbers for its longitude. Using these numbers, the location of a place can be found on a map.

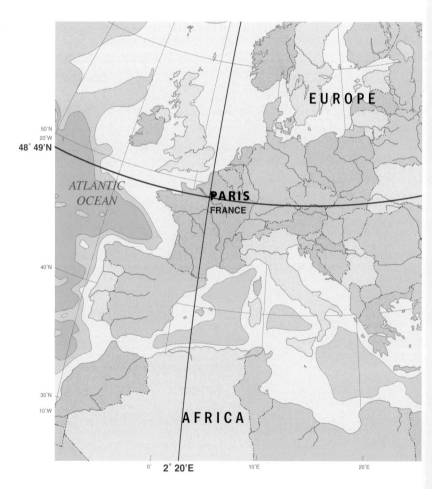

The latitude of Paris, France, is 48° 49' N. The longitude of Paris is 2° 20' E. Can you find this point on the map?

Locating Cities using Latitude and Longitude

Use the latitude and longitude lines on the map below to find the locations of cities around the world.

1. 29° 52' N, 31° 20' E
2. 34° 35' S, 58° 29' W
3. 38° 54' N, 77° 02' W
4. 11° 33' N, 104° 51' E
5. 36° 47' N, 10° 12' E
6. 53° 22' N, 6° 21' W

Answers: 1.) Cairo, Egypt 2.) Buenos Aires, Argentina 3.) Washington, D.C., United States 4.) Phnom Penh, Cambodia 5.) Tunis, Tunisia 6.) Dublin, Ireland

Reference Points

Reference points are guides or indicators that help you find locations. On a map, the most important reference points are the equator, the prime **meridian**, and the lines of longitude and latitude.

The equator is an imaginary line that circles around the center of Earth from east to west. It is the same distance from both the North and the South Pole. On a map, the equator is the 0 degree latitude line. Parts of Earth that are north of the equator are part of the northern hemisphere. Those that are south of the equator are in the southern hemisphere.

Two other imaginary latitude lines are important reference points. The Tropic of Cancer is found 23° 27' N of the equator. At noon on the first day of summer in the northern hemisphere, the Sun is directly overhead at the Tropic of Cancer. The Tropic of Capricorn is found 23° 27' S of the equator. When the Sun is directly overhead at the Tropic of Capricorn at noon, it is the first day of summer in the southern hemisphere.

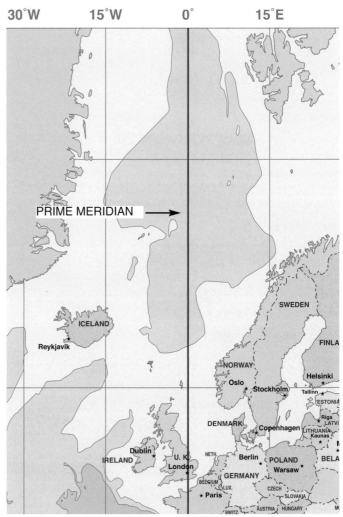

The prime meridian is an imaginary line that runs from the North to the South Poles. On a map, it is the 0° longitude line. The prime meridian separates the eastern hemisphere and the western hemisphere. It is located in Greenwich, England. Europe, Australia, Asia, and Africa are in the eastern hemisphere. North and South America are in the western hemisphere.

Locating Reference Points on a Map

The following map shows some of Earth's reference points.
Can you match the point with the correct location on the map?

1. North Pole
2. South Pole
3. Equator

4. Prime Meridian
5. Tropic of Cancer
6. Tropic of Capricorn

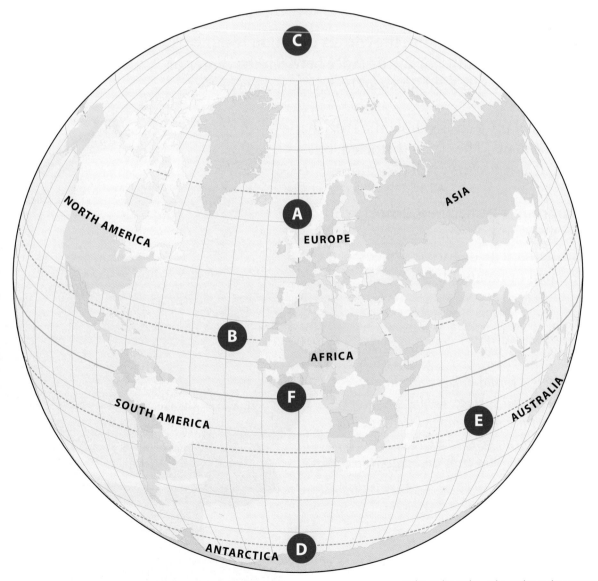

Answer: 1.) C 2.) D 3.) F 4.) A 5.) B 6.) E

Map Projections

When Earth is shown on a flat surface, such as a piece of paper, changes called distortions must be made to the way it looks. This is known as map projection. There are many types of map projections.

Equal area projections show the true size of the mapped areas when compared to the actual areas on Earth. These projections alter or distort directions and the shape of the continents.

On Azimuthal projections, the correct direction is shown. On these maps, azimuths, or the distance between the center of two points on a straight line, can be measured correctly.

Conformal projections show the true shape of the continents. The size is distorted, but the scale is the same in all directions.

Compromise projections distort directions and the shape of the continents. The distorted images are equal or balanced.

A globe is a round object that shows Earth's curved surface. Globes are more accurate than most map projections, but maps often can be used more easily. Maps can be carried on road trips and placed in books.

Recognizing Map Projections

Each type of map projection can take many forms. Research online at **http://nationalatlas.gov/articles/mapping/a_projections.html** to learn about the different types of projections and how they are used. To understand why Earth cannot be mapped correctly on a flat surface, try the following exercise.

Draw a picture on an orange. Then, carefully peel the orange so the peel remains in one complete piece. Try to lay the peel flat. What happens? Like the orange, Earth is round. When laid flat, the picture distorts.

Directions

To read a map, you must know the four cardinal, or important, points on a map. They are north, south, east, and west. There also are many intermediate points. Half cardinal points are located between two cardinal points. They are northeast, southeast, northwest, and southwest. Points located between the half cardinal points and the cardinal points are known as false points. These include north northeast and west southwest, for example.

Cardinal directions are expressed in degrees. Each of the four main points are 90° to each other. For example, north is equal to 0°, while east is equal to 90°.

A compass shows the **orientation** of a map using the cardinal points. On most maps, north appears at the top of the scale. However, it can be placed at any angle, depending on what is being shown on the map.

This compass shows cardinal and intermediate directions.

Using a Compass

A compass can help you find the location of things in your room. First, ask an adult which way is north. Then, stand so that you are facing north. Use the compass to find the location of the objects in your bedroom. For instance, your bed might be southeast, and your dresser may be west. Can you find the location of other objects in your home using the compass?

Find Buenos Aires on the map. Now, use the compass on the map pictured here to find the direction of the places listed compared to Buenos Aires.

1. Brasilia, Brazil
2. Lima, Peru
3. Santiago, Chile
4. Montevideo, Uruguay
5. Georgetown, Guyana

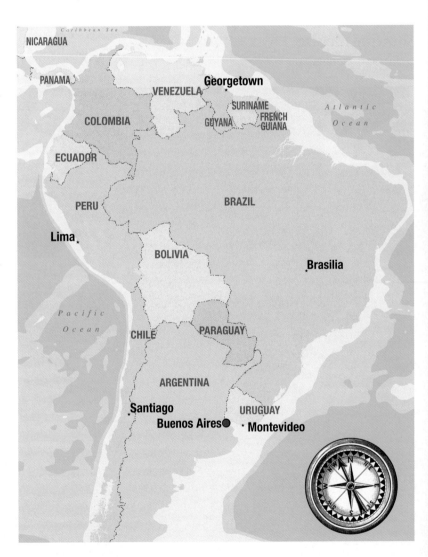

Answers: 1.) Northeast 2.) Northwest 3.) West 4.) East 5.) North

Put Your Knowledge to Use

Put your knowledge of maps to use by creating a map of your community. Begin by drawing the shape of the area on a piece of paper. Then, draw the main roads, landforms, and bodies of water. Be sure to include your house, as well as any parks, schools, stores, or other landmarks.

Once you have drawn the map, make a legend. Include all of the symbols and colors you have used to show special places on the map. Draw a compass showing direction and a scale showing the size.

Websites for Further Research

Many books and websites provide information on maps. To learn more about how to read a map, borrow books from the library, or surf the Internet.

To learn more about longitude and latitude, visit *World Atlas*.
http://worldatlas.com/aatlas/imageg.htm

Visit *nationalatlas.gov* to view maps of the United States and use an interactive mapmaker.
http://nationalatlas.gov

MapMachine has an online atlas and satellite, and thematic and physical maps to explore.
http://plasma.nationalgeographic.com/mapmachine/index.html

Glossary

archipelagos: groups of islands

atlas: a book made up of charts and maps

continents: Earth's seven main land masses; Africa, Antarctica, Asia, Australia, Europe, North America, South America

contour: outline that shows the shape or form of something

distribution: the way something is shared or spread out across an area

latitude: the distance of a place in relation to the equator

longitude: the distance of a place in relation to the prime meridian

meridian: the longitude of a particular place on Earth's surface

orientation: position or alignment

parallel: side by side at equal distances

perpendicular: to meet at a 90° angle

relief: differences in height between landforms

tectonic: relating to the processes of Earth's crust

Index